Copyright © 2020 by Daisy Ozim/Professional High Priestess

All rights reserved.

This book or any portion there of may not be reproduced or used in any manner what so ever without the express written permission of the publish except for the use of brief quotations in a book review.

Printed in the United States of America

First Printing, 2020

978-1-7349916-0-4

978-1-7349916-2-8

www.DaisyOzim.Co

TABLE OF CONTENTS

Introduction 1
What Is Tarot 2
Pathways of Analysis 8
Foundational Frameworks 12
Justification 16
Use Cases 17
Application in Legal Field 18
Federal Rules of Evidence 22
The Fair Use Act 33
Applying Tarot to Law and Litigation 35
Statistical Analysis 38
Considerations 40
Case In Point: US.Games 44
Case in Point: Co-Star, NASA & Federal Finance Laws 48
Policy Considerations 56
Conclusions 57
Knowledge Appendix 58
About The Author 61
Case Study: Ozim V. The California Endowment 62
Sources Cited 65

INTRODUCTION

Conversation regarding the use of Tarot in law is long overdue. Tarot is both a divination system as well as a metric system for the human energy field on a collective and individual level. In addition, it is backed by various systems that are rooted in empirical methodologies for ascertaining their validity. Tarot has its roots reaching back to ancient Kemet. The use of tarot over the centuries has been cloaked with folklore, mysticism as well as skepticism and ridicule. Due to historical insults such as the Crusades, Colonialism and other weapons of structural violence, tools such as tarot were demonized, limited and abused. Hence its disappearance from society. Tarot is a system that combines both the right side of the brain that drives intuition and feminine energy and the left side that drives logic and masculine energy.

The use of tarot in law acts as a balance to the injustices created by a system heavily reliant on left brained, logical and patriarchal thinking. In essence, tarot is yin to a lawyer/judges yang. The lack of consideration for tarot is rooted in Colonialism and worship of the written word which is a key aspect of White Supremacy Culture. Which poses that the written word should be worshipped at all cost. This is the logic that drove faulty scientific theories such as Eugenics. This book is designed to support existing law practitioners and individuals experiencing injustice in supporting their causes.

WHAT IS TAROT?

Tarot is a series of images depicting an archetypal theme with chronological, numerological, elemental and astrological associations. The tarot contains a categorization of all archetypes that can be expressed by the human psyche.

Through tarot, you can do the following:

Assess energetic patterns within the psyche of an individual

Psychological diagnosis tool used to translate the resonance of the archetypal patterns expressed within the psyche of an individual. Its ability to diagnosis the thoughts, intentions and actions of an individual or group as it assess the resonance generated by the thought patterns.

Empirical tool, backed by peer review, regulated frameworks backed by science to capture in real time forces working within and through an individual or group.

THE MAJOR ARCANA

The traditional tarot contains 78 cards. Other variations of tarot and oracle decks vary in number. The Major Arcana holds the keys to the main archetypes of the collective unconcious and represent major influence.
Each major Arcana is associated with a specific planetary and zodiac archetype.

THE MINOR ARCANA

The traditional tarot contains 78 cards. Other variations of tarot and oracle decks vary in number. The Major Arcana holds the keys to the main archetypes of the collective unconscious and represent major influence. Each minor arcana is associated with a specific element and planetary aspect (i.e. Sun in Virgo) that is associated with a soecific season or date.

TAROT AS A TOOL FOR ARCHETYPAL ANALYSIS

Carl Jung, one of the pioneers of western psychology was an advocate for the use of Tarot. Tarot utilizes images, numbers, colors and other forms of symbolism in order to translate archetypes. Archetypes are energetic thought patterns that are solidified within time and space and existing within the collective consciousness of all humans. As long as you have a consciousness, you are expressing an archetype. Due to tarots objective and subjective nature, it should be treated as a tool to assess the archetypal patterns operating within the consciousness of an individual.

PATHWAYS OF ANALYSIS
SUBJECTIVE OBJECTIVITY

Categorical systems rooted in science and logic such as astrological wheels allow for us to have subjective objectivity, meaning, we can assess subjective patterns customized to individuals and groups through the lens of objectivity. This happens through the understanding of archetypes. Astrology is the language of the planets and their function as archetypal forces in the constellations governed by laws of the universe. The planets correlate to astrological signs as the archetypes. All astrological signs are consecrated to an element. Fire, air, earth and water. The make up of these elements then generates a frequency as the individual or group engages in frequencies that either allow their archetype to ascend or descend. Meaning maintain a higher quality of manifestation of objective values and characteristics or maintain a manifestation of objective values and characteristics that ultimately contribute to interpersonal and societal dysfunction. The natal chart functions as a snapshot or timestamp of the planets within specific signs at the time of birth for individuals and other historical events. The natal wheel allows us to subjectively assess and measure an individual's life experience, tendencies, health status and more through the objective meaning of their planetary configuration as consecrated to a specific astrological sign and element. Individuals and generations expressing certain archetypes will produce certain objective outcomes through their subjective experiences due to the archetypal forces they maintain through their natal chart.

OBJECTIVE SUBJECTIVITY

Systems of archetype organization such as tarot allow for Objective subjectivity. This is the ability to assess subjective situations such as crimes, relationship dynamics and intentions using objective factors. Objective factors in this case include the astrological, astronomical and numerological composition of an individual as expressed through the cards. These objective factors are governed by the vibratory configuration of an individuals or groups thoughts as well as actions as they operate within the laws of frequency and vibration which are objective and measurable. Objective decision making in tarot occurs when specific cards are drawn to inquire about the specific vibratory frequency of an individual or group. The cards can categorize their actions, intentions, motives, outcomes and consequences through the composition of the cards as they translate the elemental and archetypal makeup as well as frequency of the group. This happens through the elemental, planetary and astrological breakdown of the tarot through the major and minor arcana and their definitive consecration to specific planets, astrological placements and signs and numerological correspondence with grounding in psychology and holistic health practices as previously mentioned.

Subjective Objectivity

Subjective source
Group
Individual

Objective Outcome
Associations
Chart Placements
Elemental Make Up

Tarot as Tool
of Analysis

Objective Subjectivity

Objective Source
Group
Individual

Subjective Outcome
Chart Placements
Elemental Make up

Tarot as Tool
of Analysis

FOUNDATIONAL FRAMEWORKS

To understand how tarot can act as a conduit to channel necessary information from parties involved in cases, to the development of admissible evidence, it is important to understand a few fundamental theories that each have their relevance with one another and multiple aspects of tarot.

- Universal Laws
- Human Energy Field
- Chinese Medicine
- Archetypes
- Elements and Astrology
- The Natal Wheel

The Law of Vibration

A primary law of physics and one of the 105 Universal laws, this is the atomic law of the solar system we live in that governs gravity. This Principle explains that the differences between manifestations of matter, energy, mind and spirit, result largely from varying rates in vibration. All that exists, is in constant vibration and motion. This is expressed through the states of matter, solid, liquid and gas. Every individual or group carries a specific vibration. This then generates an energy field that is enhanced or debilitated based on specific actions such as trauma, epigenetics and intrinsic as well as extrinsic factors such as pollution and nutrition. In regards to tarot, it is able to identify the frequencies of an individual or collectives thoughts, actions and future intentions. The science behind this will be discussed in detail.

Law of Vibration

Empirical
Expressed through the law of gravity as well as states of matter

Scientific
Each planet within the solar system is governed by a specific vibration and moves under its influence

Psychological
What we store within our subconscious mind is what we will manifest in our physical reality.

The Human Energy Field

Understanding the law of vibration, Each human being has a vibration they emit from their subjective energetic field. This energetic field is created through the activities of cells and tissues that generate electrical fields through the exchange of positive sodium ions and negative potassium ions to generate an energetic field that can be detected on the skin surface and through innovative technologies such as Kirilan photography. But the laws of physics demand that any electrical current generates a corresponding magnetic field in the surrounding space. Since these fields were too tiny to detect, biologists assumed they could have no physiological significance. We understand that there is a microbacterial world that we cannot see, however, we become narrow in our assumptions and ability to reason when the discussions of a macro level world that we cannot see also exists. The vibrational frequency of an individual or group iis created by the compilation of their elemental makeup. This elemental make up can dictate risk factors for illness, learning styles and more. Chinese medicine is an ancient framework for understanding the objective and measurable nature of energy, vibrations and the higher dimensional worlds that we cannot see but have access to through the translations available through tarot.

Human Energy Field

Empirical
Kirlian photography allows for the empirical assessment of human energy fields proving their existence and necessary function.

Scientific
Bioenergetics is the study of the human energy field.

Psychological
The mind emits waves ranging from delta to gamma and is influenced by intrinsic and extrinsic factor.

Archetypes

The tarot itself is a system that utilizes the science of archetypes, vibration and human energy fields. Understanding how vibratory frequencies and human energy fields is key in understanding archetypes. Archetypes are, by definition, factors and motifs that arrange the psychic elements into certain images, characterized as archetypal, but in such a way that they can be recognized only from the effects they produce. The tarot is a compilation of all archetypes that can be expressed within the human psyche. These archetypes are developed based on the objective definitions of the numerological, astrological and numerological definition each card is associated with. For instance, if I were to inquire about an individual who was a mother, the Empress, representing motherhood would come out. If I were to inquire about someone who works within the legal system, the justice card would be drawn. Jung and Frued created western psychology. Which then set the framework for the various psychological analysis tools utilized by practitioners within the field today.

Archetypes

Empirical
The theory of archetypes is evident in the development of personality tests such as Myers-Briggs.

Scientific
The solidification of energies that are constant across changing variables such as race, gender, class, etc

Psychological
The science of archetypes is also expressed within Ericksons theory of development which poses that psychological, social and moral development happens in time controlled stages.

Chinese Medicine

The power of Chinese medicine is that it takes abstract concepts that are more feminine in nature and makes them concrete through the use of logic which is masculine. Allowing the unseen to be understood in tangible ways. . It utilizes the science of the elements as they manifest through the polarities of Yin and Yang energy. Yin representing feminine energy, negative charge and the elements of earth and water. Yang representing the masculine energy, positive charge and the elements of fire and air. Chinese medicine utilizes the understanding of elements to treat illness through medical astrology. Medical astrology poses that an individual will develop certain ailments based on their elemental make up. This relates to tarot in the sense that the cards can identify individuals based on their elemental make up as well. These two systems operate out of the same exact fundamental science of elements and the archetypal forces (astrological signs) they govern.
Because Chinese medicine is an accredited health practice and recognized by the United Nations as a global practice, we can take the fundamentals of this system and utilize it to solidify the use of tarot.

Chinese medicine is rooted in the understanding of two factors. The first being Qi. This is also called life energy or vital energy. The belief is that it runs throughout your body. It's always on the move and constantly changes. This QI is none other than the human energy field that is created through the exchange of sodium and potassium ions. The quality, potency and availability of Qi within the body is governed by an individual's elemental make up, diet and exposure to external and internal traumas ranging from physical abuse to noise pollution.

CHINESE MEDICINE

Empirical
Evidence is reflected in success rate of patients who utilize TCM

Scientific
TCM is rooted in the science of Meridians which follows the same logic behind the lymphatic system

Psychological
TCM relies on the science of meridians which also mirror the nervous system

The 4 Elements and Astrology

Given our understanding of Yin, Yang and the four elements, we can now move into understanding the objective science of astrology. Because of the ways in which Western society has reduced astrology to romantic inquiry and newspaper columns, its power is untapped. Astrology is a system designed to translate the ways in which the vibrational frequencies of the planets influence human behavior, health and ancestry. The astrological wheel is separated into 12 archetypes or signs. Those archetypes are further separated by element. Each archetype is consecrated to a planetary body and the manifestation of that planetary body is explained through the Natal Chart. Archetypal forces such as planets are consecrated to each tarot card. In essence the tarot is a visionary representation of all planets and the 12 signs.

The natal chart is in direct alignment with the foundational theory of Chinese Medicine. Within a natal chart, there are 12 Houses, each house corresponds to an area of life for the individual. The specific placement of a sign within a planet and within a house will indicate the potential influences or experiences that individual will have within their lifetime.

THE FOUR ELEMENTS AND ASTROLOGY

Empirical
The four elements are reflected in the foundational theory of personality assessments

Scientific
States of matter is an equivalent.

Psychological
The four elements is used in "The Holistic System of Care for Natives in an Urban Environment designed specifically to heal trauma caused by colonization in Native American communities.

The Natal Chart

The natal chart in essence is a metric system for assessing the elemental and astrological make up of an individual. It outlines the potential manifestation of archetypal forces such as the planets in their signs as well as the influence of elements in conjunction with specific archetypal forces such as planets and the astrological sign it inhabits within a specific individual and time frame. The natal chart is in direct alignment with the foundational theory of Chinese Medicine. Within a natal chart, there are 12 Houses, each house corresponds to an area of life for the individual. The specific placement of a sign within a planet and within a house will indicate the potential influences or experiences that individual will have within their lifetime.

THE NATAL CHART

Empirical
Based on the manifestation of planetary placements on health.

Scientific
Reflected in documented accuracy of planetary influence.

Psychological
Provides deeper understanding of ones life experiences through the understanding of zodiac archetypes.

JUSTIFICATION

Each foundational framework for tarot already mentions the empirical, scientific and psychological theory associated with tarot. The following is a further explanation of uses.

Psychological

Evaluations and behavioral assesments are used often in civil and criminal litigation. Tarot is another diagnostic tool.

Empirical

Empiritcal evidence through timestamped, digital evidence outlining reoccuring patterns.

Scientific

Scientific research can be used in litigation. In this instance, the only science needed is the empirical evidence coupled with an explanation of foundational theories.

USE CASES

Tarot should be used in law for the following purposes:

Identification
The elemental configuration of an individual as consecrated to birth chart to prove association, affiliation or involvement in specific circumstances as well as nature of crimes and outcomes.

Evidence Curation
Tarot can be utilized as admissible evidence under the aforementioned fair use act and as various forms of evidence beyond testimonial. Volume 2 of this book outlines how to arrange your analysis to remain compliant with definitions of the various types of evidence.

Classification
Classification and organization of information as it relates to dates, times, seasons as well as nature of crime and outcome. Can also classify information regarding groups.

Timing
The correlation to Astrological Placements can assist in identifying specific information based on the chart listed in the KNOWLEDGE APPENDIX.

APPLICATION IN LEGAL FIELD

Tarot as A Tool for Psychological Analysis

The tarot itself is a tool to analyze and interpret the energy field and thoughts that culminate into brain wave patterns within an individual or collective. Due to the objective nature of tarot, there are virtually no ways in which to manipulate the outcome of an analysis upon a specific individual or group. Within the field of criminal justice, various evaluation mechanisms are employed in order to assess victims and perpetrators. Tarot should be considered a viable tool within the field of forensic psychology. There is a deep history around the use of Forensic Psychology in law. In this case, you as the reader/witness are the expert and do not need an advanced degree. Just a showcase of skillset. The requirements for the use of forensic psychology as evidence include a written analysis with the following:

- List of questions asked and answered during remote viewing session
- Report clearly organized with headers, titles or bullet points
- Six sources cited to create clear correlations (i.e. multiple forms of evidence, videos from the same source, consistent patterns)
- Analysis supported with clear description of card as a form of scientific body of knowledge

Tarot As Evidence

Evidence is considered to be competent and admissible if what is being presented meets some basic conditions of reliability. The showing that such evidence satisfies those tests or any conditions of admissibility is known as foundational evidence. Tarot is considered foundational evidence due to its scientific background and objectivity.

When the side opposing tarot as evidence objects to its use as not having sufficient foundation, they are actually saying that the evidence is not competent. This is false, competence is derived from reliability which lies in objectivity.

FORMS OF EVIDENCE

The proper use of tarot in law should be viewed as an enhancement versus replacement for standard forms of evidence. Tarot can be defined as the following forms of evidence:

Scientific Evidence

Scientific evidence includes any theory or body of work that has been vetted by a scientific community and become generally accepted as the truth before it will be asserted as evidence at trial. In this instance, tarot has been vetted via the aforementioned foundational theories as well as NASA via astrology. While tarot may not be widely accepted by law practitioners that is because of the lack of awareness. This does not mean it is not scientific and not acceptable. If one side of a trial wishes to submit scientific evidence that is not yet generally accepted within the scientific community, it often happens that the court orders a mini-trial to be held in order to determine the validity of the scientific theory on which the evidence is based. This body of work can suffice as evidence to prove the scientific theory behind tarot.

Forensic Evidence

There are various forms of forensic evidence including DNA, blood and psychological patterns. In this instance as tarot is a tool utilized to capture psychological archetypes in pictorial form, it can be considered a form of forensic evidence. More information on framing your tarot-as-evidence analysis is provided in further chapters.

Direct Evidence

Direct evidence is evidence of a fact based on a witness's personal knowledge or observation of that fact. In this case, one could prove a fact via an analysis and have that be direct evidence. It could then grant subpoenas which are easily accessible for further evidence. A person's guilt of a charged crime may be proven by direct evidence if, standing alone, that evidence satisfies a jury beyond a reasonable doubt of the person's guilt of that crime.

Circumstantial Evidence

Circumstantial evidence is evidence that does not directly prove guilt/innocence but expounds on any evidence previously provided that increases the likelihood of guilt/innocence. In this case, an analysis from an expert could be circumstantial evidence that leads to the discovery of direct evidence or, then allows the analysis to become direct evidence due to the facts provided.

Expert Witness Evidence

Is evidence provided by someone who is an expert within their field. The introduction of expert evidence before trial is best. It clears up unnecessary confusion, saves time and provides a stronger framework to guide the discovery process.

Corroborating Evidence

Evidence that is used to strengthen, add to, authenticate or confirm already-existing evidence is considered corroborating evidence. Tarot-as-evidence falls under this category as well and can be introduced during trial by an expert or witness to strengthen the facts of the case.

Anecdotal Evidence

Is similar to testimonial evidence. This could be police reports and depositions that have yet to be cross-examined. In this instance, a tarot analysis could be submitted as anecdotal evidence and then transform into direct evidence given the scientific background. This would then invoke FRC Rule 602 which allows witnesses directly involved to testify as experts based on their level of knowledge on a subject.

Testimonial Evidence

A witness providing their account of what happened is considered testimonial. Tarot-as-evidence analysis developed on behalf of a victim or defendant involved is admissible given a few stipulations listed in the "best practices section". This testimonial can then be transferred into

Chronological Evidence

In this instance, chronological evidence is evidence that is gathered overtime and catalogs a series of events. This form of evidence when curated by an expert/witness can be considered circumstantial evidence and lead to deeper discovery which can then solidify the facts of a case.

Incupulathory Evidence
It is the opposite of Exculpatory evidence, which tends to incriminate or prove guilt. The tarot-as-evidence analysis must prove 3 things: affiliation to crime/defendants, awareness of specific details and intent to commit acts.

Exculpatory Evidence
This evidence which tends to justify or exonerate an accused person's actions. In this case, the evidence must prove 3 things: lack of affiliation, lack of incupulathory evidence (mainly intent) and lack of forensic evidence.

Demonstrative Digital Evidence: Video recordings
Demonstrative evidence includes charts, graphs, images and other visual that explain evidence. It's used to support the demonstration of evidence. In this instance, a digital video of a reading could be utilized as demonstrative evidence as long as it follows the format mentioned in further chapters.

Documentary evidence
Is evidence contained within documents. In this instance a written analysis could be considered documentary evidence. Given one attaches the copyrights for the decks and scientific basis for utilizing this method of evidence.

Statistical Evidence
Statistical evidence in this case would be proven by repetition. Repetition would then influence the confidence of the evidence, in statistics this is defined as the percentage of accuracy of a randomization of data that produces a specific number of same or similar results. In this case. this would be based on number of matching cards in timestamped analysis that has a chronological order. When a card keeps repeating in a reading it is clear that the reading is not random but the same archetypal force is a major influence in the reading.
.

ADMISSIBLE EVIDENCE

Admissible evidence is evidence that can be used during trial. The specific statutes applying to admissible evidence are the Federal Rules of Evidence. The general rule for evidence to be admissible," the evidence must be relevant) and not outweighed by countervailing considerations (e.g., the evidence is unfairly prejudicial, confusing, a waste of time, privileged, or, among other reasons, based on hearsay)."

In this case, the scientific, behavioral and empirical evidence provided through this book would solidify tarot as a form of admissible evidence.

Tarot can be classified as admissible testimonial evidence due to the following factors:
- Objective classification as outlined above.
- Copyright of the standard Rider Waite Deck under Random house and US games classifies tarot as a publication.
- Use of copyrighted material under the Fair Use Act.
-

We will outline the Federal Rules of Evidence that must be reviewed in order to avoid having your evidence dismissed in court.

9 FEDERAL RULES OF EVIDENCE THAT APPLY TO THE USE OF TAROT IN LAW

ARTICLE I. GENERAL PROVISIONS
Rule 105. Limiting Evidence That Is Not Admissible Against Other Parties or for Other Purposes

If the court admits evidence that is admissible against a party or for a purpose — but not against another party or for another purpose — the court, on timely request, must restrict the evidence to its proper scope and instruct the jury accordingly.

This means that if your evidence is submitted against someone, the judge will not allow them to submit a similar form of evidence or attempt to use that against you and the judge will notify the jury in regards to restrictions on submissions from the opposing party as well as how this evidence will be utilized. To balance out this rule, the other party should already have awareness of this form of evidence and be prepared with their various forms of evidence.

ARTICLE IV. RELEVANCE AND ITS LIMITS

401. Test for Relevant Evidence

This rule states that evidence is relevant if:
(a) it has any tendency to make a fact more or less probable than it would be without the evidence; and
(b) the fact is of consequence in determining the action.

In this instance, the tarot gets straight to the point, is able to identify and expose necessary truths and an analysis can be utilized as exculpatory or incupulathory evidence.

402. General Admissibility of Relevant Evidence

All relevant evidence is admissible, except as otherwise provided by the Constitution of the United States, by Act of Congress, by these rules, or by other rules prescribed by the Supreme Court pursuant to statutory authority.

This clause means that in order for tarot-as-evidence to be dismissed, it needs to first be proven inadmissible without bias.

403. Excluding Relevant Evidence for Prejudice, Confusion, Waste of Time, or Other Reasons

The court may exclude relevant evidence if its probative value is substantially outweighed by a danger of one or more of the following: unfair prejudice, confusing the issues, misleading the jury, undue delay, wasting time, or needlessly presenting cumulative evidence.

Again, the objective nature of tarot, coupled with its proper classification as a science and its ability to actually curtail unnecessary waste of time via hearings and discovery make it a form of evidence that is relevant enough to survive being dismissed given the guidelines for evidence development and submission are followed thoroughly.

Rule 405. Methods of Proving Character

One of the ways in which the courts will try and dismiss evidence is by proving ones character. When this is invoked, it is a lengthy process which requires unbiased evidence. Sometimes prior convictions are invoked. However, this rule leaves too much room for hearsay which is why when it is utilized to dismiss a witness or their evidence, there needs to be direct evidence as well as a proper analysis conducted by a forensic psychologist or behavioral health specialist.

ARTICLE VI. WITNESSES
Rule 602. Need for Personal Knowledge

A witness may testify to a matter only if evidence is introduced sufficient to support a finding that the witness has personal knowledge of the matter. In this case, a witness could be considered an expert based on their skillset, occupation or training with this form of science. This transforms their evidence from testimonial to demonstrative, statistical, scientific, forensic and direct evidence.

Rule 607. Who May Impeach a Witness

Any party, including the party that called the witness, may attack the witness's credibility.

Evidence of a witness's religious beliefs or opinions is not admissible to attack or support the witness's credibility. In this instance, because of the ignorance of tarot as a science and classification system, many associate it with "fortune tellers" scammers and others they deem "less worthy" in society.

Rule 608. A Witness's Character for Truthfulness or Untruthfulness

Character evidence in support of credibility is admissible under the rule only after the witness' character has first been attacked, as has been the case at common law. If your character as an expert or witness is attacked, the opposing party must provide unbiased evidence proving your lack of trustworthiness. However, given the objectiveness of tarot, it is highly likely to have your evidence dismissed based on character without bias being involved.

Rule 610. Religious Beliefs or Opinions

This clauses states that evidence of a witness's religious beliefs or opinions is not admissible to attack or support the witness's credibility. Keep in mind that tarot is free of religious influence. In this instance, because of the ignorance of tarot as a science and classification system many associate it with "fortune tellers" scammers and others they deem "less worthy" in society.

Federal Law Protections for Religious Liberty

In the event that the courts in specific states that are highly religious and still evolving, attempt to deem tarot evidence as inadmissible due to its popular use by individuals deemed "spiritual", it would be proper to invoke the Religious Liberty Law. It is well known that many judges and lawyers are apart of organizations such as the Freemason society, Skull and Bones Society and Scottish Rites Society which are all rooted in occultism yet cloaked in "Christian Science" and practice favoritism and bias based on their affiliations. American Bar Associations Rules of Judicial Conduct Rule 3.7 was enacted for this specific purpose due to the extensive history of white supremacists colluding with the court system.

While tarot is not a religious tool, it is viewed as such. This book is a tool to separate its affiliation from any religion and establish it as a system of knowledge.

ARTICLE VII. OPINIONS AND EXPERT TESTIMONY
Rule 702. Testimony by Expert Witnesses

According to FRC, a witness is qualified as an expert by knowledge, skill, experience, training, or education. A witness can also be an individual directly involved in the court proceedings as a Plaintiff. In this case, tarot evidence from a reader who has more than 8 hours of video could be considered an expert. In addition, the utilization of this book or study of any of the bodies of knowledge that tarot is rooted in make them an expert as well. They may then testify in the form of an opinion (i.e. video or written analysis) or otherwise if:

- the expert's scientific, technical, or other specialized knowledge will help the trier (lawyer/judge/jury) of fact to understand the evidence or to determine a fact in issue;
- the testimony is based on sufficient facts or data;
- the testimony is the product of reliable principles and methods; and
- the expert has reliably applied the principles and methods to the facts of the case.

In this instance, tarot as evidence can be cultivated by a witness who has a track record of accuracy but it could also come from the plaintiff or victim as a witness as well and considered Testimonial evidence.

ARTICLE VIII. HEARSAY

FRC Rules 801-807 dictate ways in which evidence becomes inadmissible due to Hearsay. Hearsay is considered evidence received via communication from a 3rd party who submitted their testimony as witness evidence. In this case, an expert providing insight via a tarot reading would not have their analysis deemed hearsay as they are removed from the situation and solely providing an analysis on the situation.

However, a plaintiff or defendant directly involved would not have their analysis/ evidence deemed hearsay for the following reasons:

- The analysis/evidence is not offered as the truth, it is offered as evidence to prove what is argued as true
- One can put an out of court statement into evidence if the purpose is not to prove the truth of the out of court statement but to prove what was heard or seen directly.

ARTICLE IX. AUTHENTICATION AND IDENTIFICATION

Rule 901. Authenticating or Identifying Evidence

In regards to the tarot, in order for your tarot-as-evidence analysis to be authenticated and admissible in court it must be authenticated under the specific rules as an ANCIENT DOCUMENT. This rule includes following:

(8) Evidence About Ancient Documents or Data Compilations. For a document or data compilation, evidence that it:

(A) is in a condition that creates no suspicion about its authenticity;

(B) was in a place where, if authentic, it would likely be; and

(C) is at least 20 years old when offered.

The original is not necessary as long as it has the same format as the original system which they all do given the original copyrights under the Berne Convention from the early 1900s.

In addition to the aforementioned stipulations under Rule 901 section 8, section 9 is also a pathway for validating tarot-as-evidence. This states that:

(9) Evidence About a Process or System

Evidence describing a process or system and showing that it produces an accurate result.

Tarot is a classification system rooted in various sciences as is discussed here in length, in order to authenticate this evidence, one must outline its scientific background. The accuracy of the results are further outlined in its ability to properly identify isolated incidents, groups, individuals and their connection or lack thereof to each other.

Rule 902. Evidence That Is Self-Authenticating
Rule 902 states that evidence is automatically admissible and authenticated when it meets certain requirements. In this case, the following apply to tarot:

(9) Commercial Paper and Related Documents. Commercial paper, a signature on it, and related documents, to the extent allowed by general commercial law.
In this case, trademarks, patents and copyrights as well as specific user agreements with Government institutions can constitute as commercial documents.

(13) Certified Records Generated by an Electronic Process or System.
A record generated by an electronic process or system that produces an accurate result, as shown by a certification of a qualified person that complies with the certification requirements of Rule 902 (11) or (12).
The proponent must also meet the notice requirements of Rule 902 (11).

In this case, any digital videos created and uploaded online can be re-recorded via screen share and sent via a USB drive and submitted via the appendix section of a legal filing. A certification letter signed by a notary whom witnessed you fill out the documents is necessary. A notary is easily accessible online.

In addition, requirements mandated by Rule 902 section 11 as well as rule 803 Section 6 must also be met in order to have your evidence be labeled "self-authenticating" and automatically admissible. This means you would need records of a regularly conducted activity and have them notarized as well. This is as simple as making sure you have atleast 8+ hours of engagement with developing tarot as evidence via reading, developing content and supporting others with evidence development.

Rule 803 Section 6 states:
A certificate of records of a regularly conducted activity include:

A record of an act, event, condition, opinion, or diagnosis if:
(A) the record was made at or near the time by — or from information transmitted by — someone with knowledge;
*This means regularly developing analysis that are unedited following the guidelines listed here.

(B) the record was kept in the course of a regularly conducted activity of a business, organization, occupation, or calling, whether or not for profit;
*meaning you do not have to do this as a job but facilitated this act as an expert or witness as a form of evidence management
(C) making the record was a regular practice of that activity;
*this means that the development of summaries and analysis as a regular part of developing tarot-as-evidence videos or write-ups is easily proven
(D) all these conditions are shown by the testimony of the custodian or another qualified witness, or by a certification that complies with Rule 902(11) or (12) or with a statute permitting certification; and
(E) the opponent does not show that the source of information or the method or circumstances of preparation indicate a lack of trustworthiness.
*This requires simply having your certificate of authenticity with a log of your evidence notarized either in person (Rule 902 section 11) or online (Rule 902 section 13).

FAIRNESS MECHANISMS

It is clear that there are forces put in place to keep this system of injustice running. Tarot is a powerful tool that can help people achieve justice, save tax payer dollars and reduce time spent on cases. Many will not want these changes so in order to make sure your evidence is accepted bias, here are some laws and codes of conduct you can invoke.

Equal Protection Laws
Equal Protection refers to the idea that a governmental body may not deny people equal protection of its governing laws. The governing body state must treat an individual in the same manner as others in similar conditions and circumstances. If this is not the case for your evidence, you can invoke the following:

The Fourteenth Amendment
The Equal Protection Clause requires states to practice equal protection when it comes to rights provided by the government. In this, it is a right to have a fair, unbiased judge. If this is not the case, you can invoke this clause.

Selective Enforcement
Selective Enforcement occurs when government institutions fail to equally enforce the laws fail to exercise impartiality. In order to avoid this, you can invoke the following:

28 U.S. Code § 144 - Bias or Prejudice of Judge
Whenever a party to any proceeding in a district court makes and files a timely and sufficient affidavit that the judge before whom the matter is pending has a personal bias or prejudice either against him or in favor of any adverse party, such judge shall proceed no further therein, but another judge shall be assigned to hear such proceeding. In addition to this federal law, you can invoke the following codes as set forth by the American Bar Association.

Codes to Invoke Judge Accountability
Rule 2.2: Impartiality and Fairness
A judge shall uphold and apply the law,* and shall perform all duties of judicial office fairly and impartially.*

Rule 2.4: External Influences on Judicial Conduct

(B) A judge shall not permit family, social, political, financial, or other interests or relationships to influence the judge's judicial conduct or judgment.

Rule 2.6: Ensuring the Right to Be Heard

(A) A judge shall accord to every person who has a legal interest in a proceeding, or that person's lawyer, the right to be heard according to law.*

Rule 2.8: Decorum, Demeanor, and Communication with Jurors

(B) A judge shall be patient, dignified, and courteous to litigants, jurors, witnesses, lawyers, court staff, court officials, and others with whom the judge deals in an official capacity, and shall require similar conduct of lawyers, court staff, court officials, and others subject to the judge's direction and control.

Rule 2.11: Disqualification

(1) The judge has a personal bias or prejudice concerning a party or a party's lawyer, or personal knowledge* of facts that are in dispute in the proceeding.

TO CONSIDER

Now that we have covered the type of evidence tarot is classified as as well as the Federal Rules of Court governing the utilization of tarot as evidence, there are a few scenarios to consider that the judge or opposing party could invoke in order to dismiss your evidence. In order to have your evidence considered admissible and you as a witness or expert considered competent, it is important to consider the following legal frameworks that are often invoked to dismiss evidence.

Cross Examination

Cross-examination occurs when the opposing party presents a set of questions to the witness/expert in order to dismantle their credibility or viability of the evidence. In this case, these are a set of questions you will most likely need to answer in the event that you go to trial.

6 questions you must answer:

Who developed the evidence?
As a victim or witness, your evidence is considered testimonial. As an expert your evidence is considered direct, demonstrative or scientific/forensic.

Why it was developed?
In order to further prove innocence, guilt or justify an investigation.

How do we know it is without bias?
Each card has a specific meaning, so subjective translation would only impact %5-20 of the information being translated through the configuration of the cards.

How can we prove the system is accurate?
By assessing the qualifications set forth by the Frye test.

How has the system been vetted?
By the Frye test framework and utilization of its primary foundational theory, astrology across varying sectors regulated by the government.

Reliability of Evidence: Frye Test

The Frye Test is a law rule applying to scientific evidence that states results of scientific tests or procedures are admissible as evidence only when the tests or procedures have gained general acceptance in the particular field to which they belong. Tarot is a tool in psychology which was widely accepted due to Carl Jung and its primary foundational theory, Astrology is widely accepted as NASA as they sell algorithms for astrological transits to private companies.

Evaluation of Expert Status: Witness As The Expert

One way biased judges and opposing parties who will do anything to win in court is deem the witness expert as not "qualified" please keep in mind the aforementioned rules of court that consider the witness as expert of their own experience. Testimonial evidence is one of the only forms of proof that does not need reinforcing evidence for it to be admissible in court. In many criminal or civil proceedings, testimonial evidence is almost guaranteed to feature at some point in the trial.

A competent witness has to satisfy four requirements:
- They must be under oath or any similar substitute
- They must be knowledgeable about what they are going to testify.
- This means they must have perceived something with their senses that applies to the case in question
- They must have a recollection of what they perceived
- They must be in a position to relate what they communicated

Anyone inquiring about the situation through the tarot can be considered competent as they have no ability to influence the objectivity of the cards that are drawn.

THE FAIR USE ACT

Section 107 of the Copyright Act allows the utilization of copyrighted works in whole or in part as a form of evidence. Courts look at how the party claiming Fair Use is using the copyrighted work, and are more likely to find that nonprofit educational and noncommercial uses are fair. The judge must balance the purpose and character of the use utilizing the specific framework outline below:

Nature of the Copyrighted Work:

This factor analyzes the degree to which the work that was used relates to copyright's purpose of encouraging creative expression. Thus, using a more creative or imaginative work (such as a novel, movie, or song) is less likely to support a claim of a fair use than using a factual work (such as a technical article or news item). In addition, use of an unpublished work is less likely to be considered fair *Tarot is not an imaginative work. It is a taxonomic system that translates the astronomical, astrological, numerological and element configuration of individuals and groups involved in specific situations. Amount and substantiality of the portion used in relation to the copyrighted work as a whole: Under this factor, courts look at both the quantity and quality of the copyrighted material that was used. If the use includes a large portion of the copyrighted work, fair use is less likely to be found; if the use employs only

Amount and substantiality of the portion used in relation to the copyrighted work as a whole:

Under this factor, courts look at both the quantity and quality of the copyrighted material that was used. If the use includes a large portion of the copyrighted work, fair use is less likely to be found; if the use employs only a small amount of copyrighted material, fair use is more likely. That said, some courts have found use of an entire work to be fair under certain circumstances. And in other contexts, using even a small amount of copyrighted work was determined not to be fair because the selection was an important part—or the "heart"—of the work. Use of spreads, clarifies, 78 cards, 10 cards can tell a story. . .

Effect of the use upon the potential market for or value of the copyrighted work:

Here, courts review whether, and to what extent, the unlicensed use harms the existing or future market for the copyright owner's original work. In assessing this factor, courts consider whether the use is hurting the current market for the original work (for example, by displacing sales of the original) and/or whether the use could cause substantial harm if it were to become widespread. None at all, deck sold freely. The use is for the purpose of objective assessment and categorization.

The Purpose and Character of Use

The purpose of the use of evidence is also an important factor. Courts mainly deem evidence admissible when the copyrighted work is used for the purpose of criticism, news reporting, or commentary. The character of this use can be deemed "in the public interest" and are favored by the courts. In regards to tarot, the purpose is to provide commentary as an expert or testimonial as a witness which is acceptable. The character of the use is to provide a transformative form of evidence and it is also a form of news reporting which is a First Amendment right with an objective body of knowledge.

Transformative Uses

Additionally, "transformative" uses are more likely to be considered fair. Transformative uses are those that add something new, with a further purpose or different character, and do not substitute for the original use of the work. In this case, the utilization of tarot in law is a transformative use as it seeks to translate objective subjectivities and subjective objectivities through a copyrighted work as it relates to individuals/groups and their intentions, actions and motives as explained through the archetype categorization system.

APPLYING TAROT TO LAW AND LITIGATION

In order to properly apply tarot to the field of law and develop proper evidence, you must invoke the following practices and abilities:

Remote viewing

Remote viewing is essential the professional title for the utilization of psychic, telepathic and extrasensory abilities. Known as Grill Flame Protocol, special trainings were conducted to affirm an individuals abilities to be as objective as possible to be utilized by the United States government. It is important to understand RV protocol and vernacular while providing tarot as evidence services in order to further legitimize your evidence.

Intuition

Intuition and intuitive abilities are regulated by 3 systems, prefrontal cortex, enteric nervous systemic and parasympathetic nervous systems. These are necessary in order to transcend the basic meaning of the cards and tamp deeper into the analysis. Intuition is objective, you do not see/hear what you want. You see/hear what is. Intuitive abilities can be enhanced with meditation, herbal works and natural supplements such as L-Theanine.

Organization of Reading

It is important as a provider or developer of tarot-as-a-form of evidence, a consistent mechanism for developing your evidence is necessary. The following will suffice:
- A copyrighted tarot deck, mainly the Rider-Waite Deck
- Count out each card in the deck and show it clearly in order to avoid accusations of increasing the confidence interval by having multiple of the same card in one deck
- A well light table with a clear view of your hands, the spread and surrounding

- A consistent collection of data via time stamping
- Clear pronunciation of the names of all parties involved and clear descriptions with accurate correlations of any names or "clues" that arise intuitively.
- In-depth description of cards that have specific correlations to legal system/criminal activity

Time Stamping

Time stamping involves properly gathering evidence via videos or photo of spreads with write-ups at a frequency necessary to showcase the changes or consistency of the situation and the individuals/groups involved. Time Stamping does the following and requires the following:

A digital stamp of the photos taken, usually found in the "information" part of a mobile photo or by right clicking on a computer.

A clear statement of the time and date as well as location wherein the reading is taking place

An accurate file of the readings labeled in order

Spreads

A visual of a traditional tarot spread is above. Spreads helps to organize the reading, isolate the archetypes that arise in the remote viewing session and provides a foundation for a consistent method of utilizing tarot as evidence that legitimizes your remote viewing sessions and intuitive abilities as a key witness/ expert.

There are 4 concepts to understand in spreads:
- The explanation of each card as it relates to subjectivity (i.e natal chart)
- Clarification of cards that relate to varying situations and clearly state how it relates via the card
- Outlining what each card means
- Explaining the spread ahead of time. (i.e:we are going to pull 3 cards on Jane Doe to look into Situation A.)

Sample Methodology

Here is a succinct summarization of how to develop a proper case file of evidence for court utilizing tarot analysis.

STEP 1: Organize Your Tools
STEP 2: Develop Routine for Gathering Evidence
STEP 3: Submit Statistical Analysis After Every Recording via Google Drive or stored via a cloud platform
STEP 4: Certify records and recordings via notary
STEP 5: Consult with legal team for any loopholes, pitfalls or unexpected stipulations
STEP 6: Prepare for Cross-Examination & or Character Assessment

Having a checklist that you attach to every docket of evidence is also a great way to further solidify your role as an expert.

STATISTICAL ANALYSIS

A statistical analysis includes a write up of all the cards utilized within a reading and listing out the frequency of which the card had appeared. This is to prove that the cards are analyzing a specific frequency via mental archetypes (as explained previously) that are pointing towards certain actions, intents or outcomes.

Example 1

Statistical Analysis #1
Case Identifier: Jane Doe (Plaintiff),Case #, etc
Date: 2/21/20 at 1:00pm
Total Cards Drawn: 19

Cards Pulled	Frequency	Evidence
8 of Swords	2	1:02 5:28
7 of Swords	4	1:05 6:53 8:13 9:17 10:33
Justice	2	2:41 4:18
Death Card	1	3:21
5 of Wands	2	3:15 5:55
Moon	2	7:38
Queen of Wands	2	8:38 4:41
Page of Swords	2	3:05

Statistical Analysis #2
Case Identifier: Jane Doe (Plaintiff),Case #, etc
Date: 3/2/20 at 1:00pm
Total Cards Drawn: 17

Cards Pulled	Frequency	Evidence
Hierophant	1	1:13 6:22
8 of Swords	2	7:33 3:14
7 of Swords	2	2:55
Justice	3	6:05 10:09 8:35
10 of Swords	1	8:18
3 of Pentacles	2	10:15 9:46
The Tower	3	2:23
Page of Pentacles	1	9:38 4:19
Knight of Wands	2	6:27

Here is a simple method to organize the data garnered from your analysis in order to showcase frequency. This is a simple example of how your statistical analysis should be organized. In addition, a summary including the type of cards and the frequency should be included as well.

Statistical Analysis: Summary
Case Identifier: Jane Doe (Plaintiff),Case #, etc
Dates: 2/21/20 at 5:00pm, 3/2/20 at 1:00pm

Card Categories	Cards	Frequency
Justice System	Justice Hierophant 8 of Swords	10
Finances	3 of Pentacles Page of Pentacles	2
Dishonesty	7 of Swords 10 of Swords	9
Guilty Individuals	Page of Swords Queen of Wands	4
Exposure	Moon Tower Page of Swords	6
Collusion	3 of Pentacles 10 of Swords	3
Evidence	Page of Swords	5
Violence	5 of wands Knight of Wands Tower Death	8

An example of how you should summarize your statistical analysis to further validate your evidence.

Data Visualization

Below is a visualization of the summary of data. Further proving the validity of the evidence and providing another conduit that is justifiable in court as admissible evidence under the rules of demonstrative evidence.

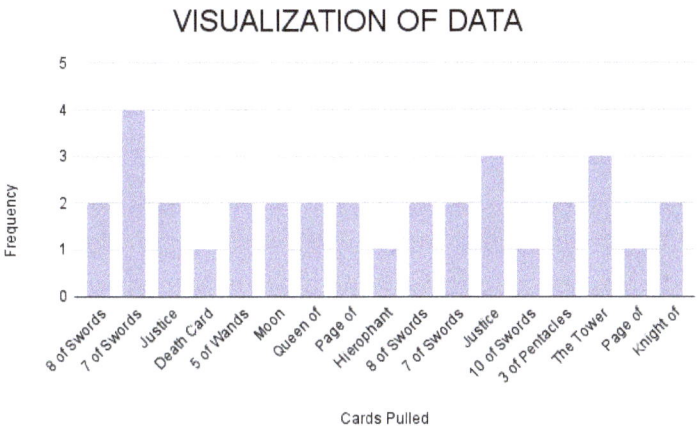

Here we see the visualization of the data to showcase the frequency. This helps to justify the specificity of the analysis to avoid having the evidence curated, labeled as random.

The best visualization methods include:
Percentage bars
Stacked Bar Graph
Multilayer pie chart
Table
Donut Chart
In addition, it is wise to have a written analysis attached as an expert. In forensic psychology, these reports are required for any analysis to be deemed admissible as evidence. It is wise to have a description of the cards with citations to various card decks that are copyrighted attached.

CONSIDERATIONS

Using only Rider Waite Deck
As this is the only deck protected under copyright law.

Timestamping
To assess changes in thoughts, patterns and behaviors before and after certain actions to assess changes via phonography and other methods deemed acceptable under the Fair Use Doctrine.

Birth chart
When assessing suspects and other parties involved, it is important to also assess the entire birth chart versus the primary sun sign. This ensures you are capturing the accurate individuals facilitating the correct corresponding actions, thoughts and intentions.

Education
Courts evaluate fair use claims on a case-by-case basis, and the outcome of any given case depends on a fact-specific inquiry. This means that there is no formula to ensure that a predetermined percentage or amount of a work—or specific number of words, lines, pages, copies—may be used without permission. This is where education comes in. Lawyers, prosecutors and judges must begin to learn and utilize tarot in their litigation process. Learning the tarot is simple and there is a standardized method due to its foundation in Chinese medicine and elemental theory. Systems of thought that have high relevance in medicine, academia and research.

Proper Use
The proper use of tarot in law should be viewed as an addition versus replacement for research, interviews and the standard litigation process.

Developing Accurate Assessments

In order to make sure the most accurate information is derived from a tarot assessment, it is wise to inquire about the individual or incident at hand on at least 3 different occasions. The reoccurring cards indicate the overall energy the individual or incident is emanating.

Gender Based Cards

Various cards represent the vibrational frequency of gender. Because gender exists on an energetic spectrum, those who may embody a masculine physical form can show up as a feminine figure within a card analysis. Developing Accurate Assessments In order to make sure the most accurate information is derived from a tarot assessment, it is wise to inquire about the individual or incident at hand on at least 3 different occasions. The reoccurring cards indicate the overall energy the individual or incident is emanating.

ADDITIONAL TOOLS

While tarot is the main tool you can use that is legally justifiable as self- authenticating evidence, you can utilize a few specific tools to enhance the reading. They are as follows:

Regular Decks

While these cards are mainly used for games, they can be used as clarifiers since it is only the minor arcana included w/the fool card (joker).

Gypsy Oracle

This deck is one of the first decks copyrighted under the Berne Convention and useful for digging deeper in readings.

Kipper Deck

The Kipper deck is good for isolating individuals involved as well as current actions. Should always be used as a clarifier.

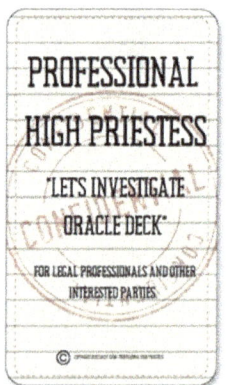

Photographic Memory Deck

For those still learning to read tarot, this has an accurate pictorial representation of what each card means as well as definitions for easy learning specific for those in the legal field.

CASE IN POINT: SOLIDIFYING LEGALITY OF TAROT AS EVIDENCE

The following are two examples of the ways in which tarot and astrology, which is directly connected to the tarot have been involved in various systems of litigation and finance in order to generate profit for international companies.

These examples should be used to further expose the fallacies, double speak and double standard applied to these practices when they are dismantling systems of injustice.

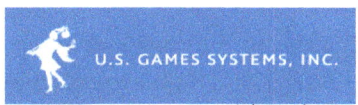

U.S. Games owns a copyright on the original tarot through Random House and will be analyzed as an example.

Co-Star

A corporation which is regulated by the SEC and currently going public via IPO will be analyzed here as well.

The United States Playing Card Company

Owns trademarks and copyrights to card systems classified as "scientific" under their United States Trademark Application

EXAMPLE: US GAMES & US PLAYING CARD COMPANY

The first copyrights for tarot were legitimized via the Berne Convention in the United Kingdom. The Berne Convention, adopted in 1886, deals with the protection of works and the rights of their authors. It provides creators such as authors, musicians, poets, painters etc. with the means to control how their works are used, by whom, and on what terms. The Rider-Waite Tarot cards are subject to UK copyright laws because the works were first published in the UK. The copyright term is 70 years from date of death of the author. They were then republished in the US by Random House Games.

These decks were not used for "gaming" purposes, they were utilized by the elite as forms of divination spearheaded by the Golden Dawn Society.

Below is an excerpt from the initial copyright

"The copyright owner is J. D. Semken, the surviving executor of W. R. Semken who died in July 1970. He was one of two ultimate residuary legatees under the will of Arthur Edward Waite, who died on 19 May 1942. After the death on 15 September 1980 of Miss A. S. M. Waite, the tenant for life, the Public Trustee, in winding up the Waite estate, assigned to W.R. Semken and J. D. Semken "all the copyright and rights in the nature of copyright in the works of Arthur Edward Waite comprised in his estate".

"Random House: Publish the cards under an exclusive license from the copyright owner.

"The Rider-Waite cards were first published in 1910 under exclusive license by A. E. Waite's publisher Rider & Co and were subsequently republished by the successors of Rider & Co, Hutchinson Publishing Group and in 1993 with J. D. Semken's full agreement by Random House under the Rider imprint.

US Games: Effectively a sub-licensee of Random House and holder of Rider-Waite trademarks throughout the world. Publishing history of cards."

The excerpt above outlines tarots legality as a copyrighted tool. Since then, the primary company providing copyrights for Tarot Decks, US Games has trademarked the company under class 42 of the International Class system.

Class 42: Computer and Software Services and Scientific Services

Scientific and technological services and research and design relating thereto; industrial analysis and research services; design and development of computer hardware and software.

Pseudo Mark	US GAMES

Classification Information

International Class	42 - Scientific and technological services and research and design relating thereto; industrial analysis and research services; design and development of computer hardware and software; legal services. - Scientific and technological services and research and design relating thereto; industrial analysis and research services; design and development of computer hardware and software; legal services.
US Class Codes	100, 101
Class Status Code	6 - Active
Class Status Date	1999-05-10
Primary Code	042

Correspondences

Name	THOMAS J MOORE
Address	*Please log in with your Justia account to see this address.*

Source: Justia.com

This is a clear indication that the creators, sellers and copyright holders of dozens of tarot decks understand what this tool is and have since submitted documentation to classify their companies as providers of scientific research and tools.

Another company that copyrights a similar card system which is the 52 card deck of only the major arcana and the Joker (better known as the Fool card) is listed under Class 9 of the international Class System.

Class 9: Computer and Software Products and Electrical and Scientific Products

Scientific, nautical, surveying, photographic, cinematographic, optical, weighing, measuring, signaling, checking (supervision), life-saving and teaching apparatus and instruments; apparatus and instruments for conducting, switching, transforming, accumulating, regulating or controlling electricity; apparatus for recording, transmission or reproduction of sound or images; magnetic data carriers, recording discs; automatic vending machines and mechanisms for coin operated apparatus; cash registers, calculating machines, data processing equipment and computers; fire extinguishing apparatus.

Pseudo Mark	BEE

Classification Information

International Class	9 - Scientific, nautical, surveying, electric, photographic, cinematographic, optical, weighing, measuring, signalling, checking (supervision), life-saving and teaching apparatus and instruments; apparatus for recording, transmission or reproduction of sound or images; magnetic data carriers, recording discs; automatic vending machines and mechanisms for coin-operated apparatus; cash registers, calculating machines, data processing equipment and computers; fire-extinguishing apparatus. - Scientific, nautical, surveying, electric, photographic, cinematographic, optical, weighing, measuring, signalling, checking (supervision), life-saving and teaching apparatus and instruments; apparatus for recording, transmission or reproduction of sound or images; magnetic data carriers, recording discs; automatic vending machines and mechanisms for coin-operated apparatus; cash registers, calculating machines, data processing equipment and computers; fire-extinguishing apparatus.
US Class Codes	021, 023, 026, 036, 038
Class Status Code	2 - Sec. 8 - Entire Registration
Class Status Date	2010-07-24

Source:Justia.com

The classification of their products and services as "scientific tools" is in alignment with the justifications aforementioned which solidify tarot as a science based system.

Given the two examples above, it is clear the creators and manufacturers behind these systems are aware of their proper use.

There are more fallacies to further highlight within the United States Justice System regarding their impartiality and double speak when it comes to the utilization of these tools.

One could say that these companies are only protecting their artwork, however the applications covers images, numbers and meaning. Both the literary and pictorial aspects of these bodies of work are protected under USPTO laws.

The following laws also apply here:

17 U.S. Code § 409 - Application for Copyright Registration

Applying to both copyrights, patents and trademarks, this law poses that any individual or corporation that wants protections, which is considered a benefit from the United States Government must fill out the documentation and provide all accurate information.

This then invokes:

18 U.S. Code § 506 - Seals of departments or agencies

This law states that a violation consists of (1) a false representation; (2) of a material fact; (3) was knowingly made; (4) in a copyright/trademark or patent application or any written statement filed in connection with an application. This basically states that any falsification of documentation submitted can result in legal ramifications. Oddly, these companies and several others renew their licenses with the government every 10-20 years and they are reviewed by humans. Meaning the United States government is aware of the primary classification and application of these tools.

This means the entire USPTO system needs to reclassify these tools under Class 9 and 41, 42 respectively in order to avoid further duplicity.

EXAMPLE: CO-STAR

The aforementioned scientific and psychological basis of astrology cannot be dismissed when discussing the tarot. As an example, we will further legitimize tarot as well as astrology by examining the company Co-Star which has investors and is in the process of registering to become a publicly traded company. This can be used as a form of evidence when justifying your use of tarot. This company is classified as the following:

Classification Information

International Class	009 - Scientific, nautical, surveying, electric, photographic, cinematographic, optical, weighing, measuring, signalling, checking (supervision), life-saving and teaching apparatus and instruments; apparatus for recording, transmission or reproduction of sound or images; magnetic data carriers, recording discs; automatic vending machines and mechanisms for coin-operated apparatus; cash registers, calculating machines, data processing equipment and computers; fire-extinguishing apparatus. - Scientific, nautical, surveying, electric, photographic, cinematographic, optical, weighing, measuring, signalling, checking (supervision), life-saving and teaching apparatus and instruments; apparatus for recording, transmission or reproduction of sound or images; magnetic data carriers, recording discs; automatic vending machines and mechanisms for coin-operated apparatus; cash registers, calculating machines, data processing equipment and computers; fire-extinguishing apparatus.
US Class Codes	021, 023, 026, 036, 038
Class Status Code	6 - Active
Class Status Date	2019-05-16
Primary Code	009
First Use Anywhere Date	2017-07-00
First Use In Commerce Date	2017-07-00
International Class	045 - Personal and social services rendered by others to meet the needs of individuals; security services for the protection of property and individuals. - Personal and social services rendered by others to meet the needs of individuals;

Source:Justia.com

According to their trademark filing and the many copyrights they have on information that belongs within the public domain. they are in essence providing a science based tool that has physical and behavioral health implications. However they do not have the necessary licenses and classifications as needed by the following federal agencies which regulate them:

NASA

NASA is one out of the 3 primary partnerships that allow this platform to function. We will provide an overview of the clauses which implicate the government in hiding the use of astrology/tarot as a powerful tool backed by science yet utilizing personal astrology data for research purposes.

Affiliations

Co-Star utilizes data that NASA is funded to collect on current planetary transits (aka communications between planets and zodiac signs), asteroid movements and constellation data. This data is considered by NASA to be scientific data which it is and since they are funded by tax payer dollars, should be available to the public domain.

THE HYPER-PERSONALIZED, SOCIAL ASTROLOGY EXPERIENCE.

Co-Star.

Most horoscopes ask what month you were born. Co-Star asks what minute.
Powered by AI that merges NASA data with the insight of human astrologers.

DOWNLOAD IOS   DOWNLOAD ANDROID

Source:Costar.com

Data Agreements

NASA has 4 data agreements (8 agreements in total) which govern the use of its data for 3rd parties. Here, we will review two agreements which ascertain Astrology as a science and not a form of entertainment or baseless practice. Co-Star utilizes the following two.

The Standard Nonreimbursable patent and invention rights sample clause 1.2.d.d. in appendix 1 is to be used in agreements for joint activities (i.e., each party funding its own agreed-to activities), wherein NASA may perform research, experimental, developmental, engineering, demonstration, or design work of the type that could result in inventions being made in carrying out activities under the agreement. In this situation, the principle that each party keeps rights to their own intellectual property still applies, except that as an incentive to commercialize NASA-developed technology, NASA will use reasonable efforts to grant the participant, in accordance with the requirements of 37 CFR Part 404, an exclusive or partially exclusive commercial license (on terms and conditions to be negotiated) to any NASA invention that may be made under the agreement or for any invention NASA acquires title from its contractor and, on which NASA decides to file a patent application and receives a patent.

This license to the private participant will be subject to the retention of a Government-purpose license, and a nonexclusive license to the contractor (where title is acquired from a support contractor). The commercial license to the private participant is to be royalty-bearing and revocable if the invention is not commercialized consistent with NASA (and Governmentwide) policy in licensing its inventions. It also provides an opportunity for royalty-sharing with the employee-inventor, consistent with NASA, and Governmentwide policy under the National Technology Transfer and Advancement Act (PL. 104-113), [codified as amended at 15 U.S.C. § 3710 et seq.] The foregoing will also apply to any undivided interest NASA acquires for any invention made jointly with the private participant. As to an invention made solely by the private participant, NASA generally acquires no rights whatsoever, but may, under certain circumstances, negotiate a license to use the invention for research,demonstration, test, and evaluation purposes.

Sample Clause, see appendix 1, clause 1.2.d.d. "Intellectual Property and Data Rights" Patent and Invention Rights (Nonreimbursable Space Act Agreement) Standard Form Sample Clause.

Source:NASA.COM

This specific agreement allows for NASA to utilize any data curated on the platform via their technology for their own personal research which would put NASA in violation of all the following laws and clauses listed here.

The Standard Reimbursable data rights sample clause 1.2.i.i. in appendix 1 is to be used in agreements involving research, experimental, developmental, engineering, demonstration, or design activities for which NASA is reimbursed, where it is likely that proprietary information will be developed or exchanged under the agreement. Again, the same basic protective and rights allocation scheme is provided as in the short form reimbursable clause, but with more procedural specificity to address matters that often arise when it is anticipated that proprietary information is to be developed or exchanged in any activity. Also, copyright is specifically addressed.

Sample Clause, see appendix 1, clause 1.2.i.i. "Intellectual Property and Data Rights" Rights in Data (Reimbursable Space Act Agreement) Standard Form Sample Clause.

Source:NASA.COM

This agreement clearly states that the data is to be used for specific purposes involving science and research.

Partnership Requirements

According to NASA, in order to utilize their technologies and data, you must fall in line with their "Tech Readiness Levels" and have a science backed methodology. Meaning they are aware of the science behind astrology. Co-Star in on Level 4.

TRL 1
Basic principles observed and reported
Basic scientific research that can be turned into an application or a concept under a research and development program is considered.

TRL 2
Technology concept or application formulated
An idea is proposed for the practical application of current research, but there are no experimental proofs or studies to support the idea.

TRL 3
Concept or application proven through analysis and experimentation
Active research and development begins, including analytical laboratory-based studies to validate the initial idea, providing an initial "proof of concept."

TRL 4
Basic prototype validated in laboratory environment
Basic examples of the proposed technology are built and put together for testing to offer an initial vote of confidence for continued development.

TRL 5
Basic prototype validated in relevant environment
More realistic versions of the proposed technology are tested in real-world or near real-world conditions, which includes initial integration at some level with other operational systems.

TRL 6
System or subsystem model or prototype demonstrated in a relevant environment
A near final version of the technology in which additional design changes are likely is tested in real-life conditions.

TRL 7
System prototype demonstrated in a relevant environment
The final prototype of the technology that is as close to the operational version as possible at this stage is tested in real-life conditions.

TRL 8
Actual system completed and qualified for flight through test and demonstration
The technology is thoroughly tested and no further major development of the technology is required. Its operation as intended is demonstrated without significant design problems.

TRL 9
Actual system proven through successful operation
The final operational version of the technology is thoroughly demonstrated through normal operations, with only minor problems needing to be fixed. Any further improvements to the technology at this point, whether planned or not, will be treated as a TRL 1.

Please note, these requirements are not just for aerospace machines and satellites they apply to web applications and machine learning/AI projects as well.

Privatizing Public Data
37 CFR Part 404 - Licensing Of Government-Owned Inventions

According to the Code of Federal Regulations, requirements must be met for licensing a government owned invention (NASA). This clause states that:

"A license may be granted only if the applicant has supplied the Federal agency with a satisfactory plan for development or marketing of the invention, or both, and with information about the applicant's capability to fulfill the plan. The plan for a non-exclusive research license may be limited to describing the research phase of development."

In essence, the United States Government just exposed the fact that they licensed a data and technology tool to a private company for payment while also deeming the practice nonsensical when applied to criminal and civil investigations and disputes.

Title 42 Chapter 26
Space Activities That Impact Human Health & The Utilization of Space Data in Relation to Public Health

There are public health laws that govern NASA's use of public data on the health of the public at large as well as the regulation of what data is sold, accessed privately and or utilized for research. All of those laws have since been wiped from the internet based on recent events as described in the "personal story" section.

Security Exchange Commission
Penalties for Investing in Unregulated/Unsubstantiated Technology

Co-Star, as an astrology app can be considered "unregulated" as there are no laws set forth to officiate the practice as an official health and psychology practice under the United states government. If this is the case, the company as well as their investors are violating several securities laws as they are selling shares which requires registration and review by the SEC. This means the SEC is aware that the practice is substantiated. This can easily be amended by registering Astrology as a medical and psychological practice under the AMA and APA.

Compliance Program Regulations

Investors and Investment Companies have to have specific compliance programs set forth to manage accounting of investments, staying in compliance with investment laws based on the industry they are specifically investing in.

In this case, the SEC is aware of the validity of Astrology as they allow investment firms and accredited individual investors to buy shares of the company even though it would be deemed out of compliance, high risk and an unsubstantiated/unregulated market. This means they must then affirm astrology AND tarot as a legally, academically and medically sound practice or they are in violation of their own laws.

Forward Statements as A Risk

Forward statements are considered a risk and regulated by both the SEC and FCC. Oddly, Astrology is rooted in "forward statements" and prevention. A forward statement is one that suggest something "will happen" If this is the case, the owners of the company and investors are violating certain clauses as they clearly believe in the predictive and preventive nature of astrology.

In some cases, you can identify forward-looking statements by terms such as "may," "will," "should," "would," "expect," "plan," "anticipate," "could," "intend," "target," "project," "contemplate," "believe," "estimate," "predict," "potential" or "continue" or the negative of these terms or other similar expressions.

This then calls on FCC laws on accurate communication.

HIPPA Laws

Privacy Rules for Health Clearing Houses

The Privacy Rule, applies to this app as it functions as a health care clearinghouses. The purpose is the collection and dissemination of health data which is regulated by HIPPA. This app includes the gathering of the information of others that can be utilized in health analysis via astrology. The Privacy Rule specifically applies to "individually identifiable health information" held or transmitted by a covered entity or its business associate, in any form or media, whether electronic, paper, or oral.

This form of information, includes the individual's past, present or future physical or mental health or condition. In this case, the app allows individuals to process their own data as well as the data of others unbeknownst to them and identify personal information about their physical health (1st and 6th house) and their mental health (3rd house, 12th house and Mercury).

This is basically saying that if the government and capitalism want to generate funds off of an ancient indigenous practice, they must follow all the rules and regulations of the Government regardless of the personal opinions of policy makers and other individuals who influence Astrologies and tarots accessibility within public systems.

Utilization of Health Data

The Privacy Rule defines research as, "a systematic investigation, including research development, testing, and evaluation, designed to develop or contribute to generalizable knowledge." 45 C.F.R. § 164.501. This company allows others to process their "health data" which is their placements and that of others via their platform which is not in compliance. This is to state that the United States government is out of compliance with its own system especially given the classification of related practices and tools as "scientific" and health related.

Federal Trade Commission
Health Breach Notification Rule

Health Breach Notification Rule is designed to regulate companies that are not covered by HIPPA. It states that the company must be in compliance with certain practices in order to protect health data and continue generating income as a business. Co-Star also shares data with NASA as apart of its business model. NASA requires compliance with all of the federal bodies mentioned in order to maintain this partnership. Meaning the federal government is highly aware of the power, science and application of Astrology.

Federal Lanham Act

The Federal Lanham and which is enforced by the FTC states that businesses must be accurate in their advertisement to consumers. As Astrology is an evidence based practice with a strong scientific background, the lack of proper education regarding its proper use in medicine, mental health and governance must be mentioned. This in part is to avoid misuse and abuse of data on behalf of users as well as.

15 USC § 1125 (2011)

This clause from the US Code and Stature Law States
(B) in commercial advertising or promotion, misrepresents the nature, characteristics, qualities, or geographic origin of his or her or another person's goods, services, or commercial activities.
In this case, their advertising is misleading as they are not stating explicitly that the platform is for scientific purposes that affect your physical and mental health and collects private data that is then given to the government to run experiments.

NEW YORK STOCK EXCHANGE LAWS

Requirements for Companies Providing HealthTech Platforms

It is clear that this company could be labeled as a "healthtech" company. Because this company plans to go public in the near future, which means offering shares of their company for sale to the public. As previously mentioned they are currently funded by investments. According to SEC/NYSE/HIPPA requirements for publicly traded companies, they are out of compliance as they are not a covered entity.
Because this app is considered Health Tech in the sense that it is a digital clearing house due to Astrology's roots in medicine, then this app provides a strong foundation for legitimizing this practice within the United States government which would directly impact the legal viability of tarot.
This herein part is rooted in the common senses awareness that this generates income for regulated investors who invested funds into their company and then registered this transaction with the SEC who is supposed to manage technicalities of this nature for a platform that in all actuality is geared towards health.

POLICY CONSIDERATIONS

The aforementioned examples, research, scientific data as well as case studies are necessary in developing a framework for utilizing tarot within the justice system. The following are specific policy recommendations that systems can begin implementing immediately in order to support the successful integration of these practices and practitioners.

TRAINING IN LAW SCHOOL
Legal practitioners should be provided with an in-depth training in order to support not just their clients but themselves. This can also assist in not accepting case loads wherein, their client is actually the culprit. Reducing stress and karmic debts from defending the wrong individual/group as well as supporting their clients in obtaining justice.

CERTIFIED TRAININGS
Individuals who may come from other educational or occupational backgrounds should be able to access the proper training necessary in order to provide tarot-as-evidence services. This could be likened to the court reporter system.

INCLUSION INTO THE FEDERAL RULES OF Court
The FRC section governing evidence should be updated given the examples and additional classifications of this tool outlined previously. This can help in instituting a standardized-system and stop bias amongst judges and jurors from accepting viable evidence.

TECHNOLOGY FOR STREAMLINING PROCESSES
Technology platforms that already exist can be merged with plug-ins or apps that allow individuals to upload written analysis or video evidence for easier viewing for all parties involved. This also ensures integrity when moving data from one individual to another.

CONCLUSIONS

Conversation regarding the use of Tarot in law is long overdue. Tarot is both a divination system as well as a metric system for the human energy field on a collective and individual level. Tarot has its roots reaching back to ancient Egypt. The use of tarot over the centuries has been cloaked with folklore, mysticism as well as skepticism and ridicule.Due to historical insults such as the Crusades, Colonialism and other weapons of structural violence, tools such as tarot were demonized, limited and abused. Hence its disappearance from society. Tarot is a system that combines both the right side of the brain that drives intuition and feminine energy and the left side that drives logic and masculine energy.

KNOWLEDGE APPENDIX

The following are diagrams of the foundational theories governing the legitimacy of tarot.

ZODIAC WHEEL

The zodiac wheel is the organization of all the archetypes that can be expressed within the human psyche. The Zodiac wheel is the root foundation for the Tarot Association wheel which outlines the consecration of all 78 cards to a specific planetary placement, date and season.

CHINESE MEDICINE WHEEL

The Chinese medicine wheel organizes organ systems based upon their "element" which denotes its function. The Chinese Medicine wheel is in direct alignment with the Medical Astrology Wheel which is rooted in the original Zodiac Wheel.

NATAL CHART

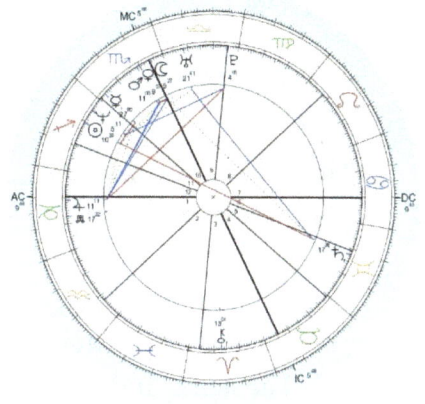

The Natal Chart is a mathematical and astronomical representation of an individual based on their time, date and location of birth. It is a relfect of ones primary element, what diseases they may be prone to as well as psychological predisposition. Ancestral/generational patterns are also relfected within the Natal Chart

MEDICAL ASTROLOGY

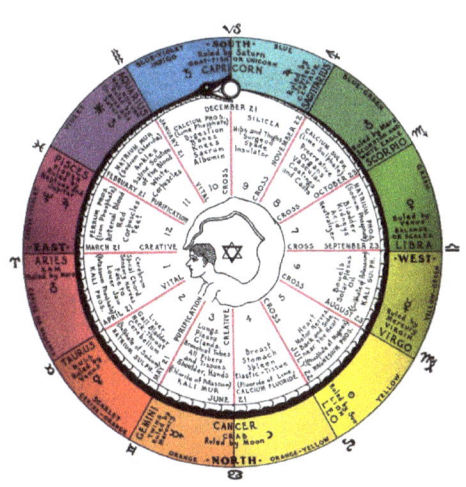

Medical Astrology is the study of ones zodiac placements upon their health. It is rooted in the theory of chinese medicine and the Tarot Planetary Association Wheel.

TAROT PLANETARY ASSOCIATION WHEEL

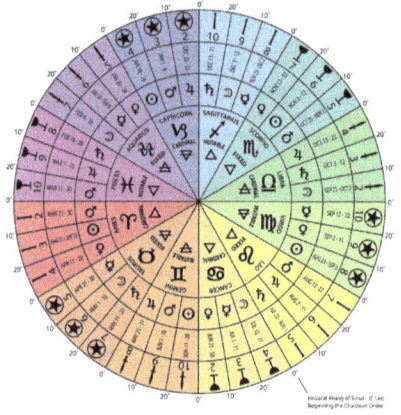

This wheel outlines the planetary placement and zodiac archetype associated with each tarot card with dates and seasons aligned with the Gregorian calendar.

ABOUT THE AUTHOR

Daisy Ozim aka Professional High Priestess is a public health educator, tech founder and public speaker. She received her education at San Francisco State University and spent years doing community advocacy work around health as well as technology. Her time is spent between education on spiritual warfare and the organization she founded to address intergenerational trauma through systems change, training and technology. Having experienced spiritual attacks that almost took her life, she is dedicated to supporting global initiatives and policy changes to address the public health impacts of evil.

PERSONAL STORY

This book arose from my own personal experience with the tarot and utilizing it over a span of 3 years to obtain justice for myself and others. While tarot readers are demonized and not taken seriously because of White Supremacy. The foundations of tarot come from Ancient Kemet, a very advanced civilization that had a physical existence on planet earth with its holographic and etheric existence in a differing galaxy. They clearly understood the body, the mind and soul in ways we cannot fathom now. So much so that they drew hieroglyphs of cells and mitosis that still exist today in a place called "Temple of Man" in Luxor.

I was stalked and harassed for over 3 years by a group of practitioners who were hired by a foundation, The California Endowment over the span of 3 years. This is because my telepathic, intuitive and remote viewing skills were a threat to one of their staff members who turned out to be a serial killer. They tried to hide the fact that the practitioners they hired were implicated in the death of 2 community members Prince White and aManda Greene who both passed at 37 within 6 months of each other from rare cancers of the endocrine system. I utilized my awareness of tarot and the legal system to organize all of the evidence on top of evidence that was found by nature of dealing with people who always get caught when justice will be served. I took this organization, The California Endowment to court for their acts against me and listed the various tarot readings as evidence.

Before the case could even make it to trial, they had it rigged due to their affiliation with the Governor for the State of California, Gavin Newsome. The first action they took was to strike the **mentioning** of this evidence and the legal evidence supporting its use from the complaint.

I attempted to conduct discovery to gather evidence which was proven by the numerous readings I conducted by invoking Federal Rules of the Court Number 9 which they again had rigged in their favor. They then filed Motion to Strike Portions of Plaintiff's Amended Complaint and specifically requested that the mentioning of the Fair Use Act and the tarot as evidence be removed.

The following is an overview of the illegal mechanisms utilized by the defendant in order to have tarot as evidence removed and hidden as a viable form of evidence in an attempted murder case.

-Messages to defendant
-Recorded phone calls
-Defendants spouse lack of income, tax returns, app store records
-Defendants spouse release records from previous employer
-Bank statements of defendant
-Bank statements , app store records, internet search records and medical records of plaintiff
-Social media records showing defendant and spouse argument after magic was exposed (proving awareness and belief yet lack of action)
-The Rider-Wait Tarot (which is the standard decks used in the testimonial videos) is copyrighted by US Games Systems.

"The copyright owner is J. D. Semken, the surviving executor of W. R. Semken who died in July 1970. He was one of two ultimate residuary legatees under the will of Arthur Edward Waite, who died on 19 May 1942. After the death on 15 September 1980 of Miss A. S. M. Waite, the tenant for life, the Public Trustee, in winding up the Waite estate, assigned to W.R. Semken and J. D. Semken "all the copyright and rights in the nature of copyright in the works of Arthur Edward Waite comprised in his estate".

"Random House: Publish the cards under an exclusive license from the copyright owner. (They do have the documentary and contract evidence to prove the position)

"US Games: Effectively a sub-licensee of Random House and holder of Rider-Waite trademarks throughout the world.

Copyrighted documents can be utilized in court cases. "The fair use doctrine allows for the use of copyrighted information for use in litigation. Reproduction of copyrighted material (Tarot cards) for use in litigation or potential litigation is generally fair use, even if the material is copied in whole

This is the initial complaint filed with forms of evidence listed.

```
 1      9.   Page 7, the entirety of the paragraph with the heading "SB 577 Section 2053.6."
 2     10.   Page 7, the entirety of the paragraph with the heading "Intentional Misrepresentation:
 3    Chapter 5 Section 2000 - Division 2 of Business and Professions Code."
 4     11.   Pages 7-8, the entire section entitled "Evidence available."
 5     12.   Page 8, the entire section again entitled "Evidence available."
 6     13.   Page 8, the entire paragraph beginning "The copyright owner..." and ending "...in his
 7    estate."
 8     14.   Page 8, the entire paragraph beginning "Random House:..." and ending "...the position)".
 9     15.   Page 8, the entire paragraph beginning ""US Games:..." and ending "...the world."
10     16.   Page 8, the entire paragraph beginning "Copyrighted documents..." and ending "...copied
11    in whole."
12
13    Dated: August 5, 2020              VOGL MEREDITH BURKE LLP
14
15                                       By: _____
16                                          E. Forrest Shryock, Jr.
17                                          Mark D. Fenske
                                            Attorneys for Defendant
18                                          THE CALIFORNIA ENDOWMENT
```

This is the defendants Motion to Strike which specifically requested the aforementioned evidence that proved tarot's legality as evidence, be removed.

This led to an international FBI investigation due to my writings on the use of spellwork which garnered $1.8 million dollars for the United Nations Witchcraft council. I utilized my skills in then helping the FBI find over 45 bodies and 19 ritualistic murders via my abilities which helped apprehend, indict and jail multiple individuals involved.

By invoking my awareness of the FAIR USE ACT, my readings on the situation were utilized to draft warrants and indictments, justify surveillance and initiate justice for thousands of people. I hope this book as well as my story and the suffering of hundreds of people at the hands of sinister individuals is rectified by integrating this system into our current system that produces more injustices than justice.

SOURCES CITED

Admissible Evidence. Federal Rules of Evidence. Legal Information Institute. Cornell Law Library. 2021

Compliance Programs of Investment Companies and Investment Advisers. 7 CFR Parts 270 and 275. Release Nos. IC-25925, IA-2107; File No. S7-03-03] RIN 3235-AI77. 2020

Fair Use Act Overview. United States Copyright Office. 2020

False designations of origin, false descriptions, and dilution forbidden. Title 15 - Commerce and Trade Chapter 22 - TRADEMARKS (§§ 1051 - 1141n) Subchapter III - GENERAL PROVISIONS (§§ 1111 - 1129) Section 1125. 2020

Forensic Report Checklist, Open Access Journal of Forensic Psychology, 2:233-240, 2021

Health Breach Notification Rule, 16 C.F.R. Part 318. 2021

Licensing of Government Owned Inventions. 37 CFR Part 404. Legal Information Institute. 2021
National Aeoronautic Space Institute. Space Act. Rules and Regulations for Data Sharing. 2021

Ozim Vs. The California Endowment. Alameda County Superior Court. DomianWeb. 2021

Operation Grill Flame. Practices and Procedures for Remote Viewer Training. CIA-RDP96-00788R000901130001-8. 2020

STARGATE PROJECT. Central Intelligence Agency. Freedom of Information Act Electronic Reading Room. 2020

The Rider Tarot deck VA 101-718 (1982). The Rider Tarot deck; trademark No. 1-644-495 (1991). The Rider-Waite tarot deck; trademark No. 1-640-623 (1991). UNITED STATES PATENT OFFICE. 2020

U.S. Games Systems, Inc. Reproduction and Usage Policies For Copyrighted Tarot Card Images. Last Rev 04/20/2017. 2020

World Intellectual Property Organization. Berne Convention for the Protection of Literary and Artistic Works. 2021.

www.ingramcontent.com/pod-product-compliance
Lightning Source LLC
Chambersburg PA
CBHW051948160426
43198CB00013B/2358